WHY VENDING MACHINES ARE NOT PASSIVE INCOME AND YOUR GUIDE TO REAL PROFIT

Matthew Woodhams

Vending Bible

To my wonderful family, thank you for your endless love, support, and encouragement to turn my passion into my work, and to the industry veterans, your shared knowledge has been invaluable.

CONTENTS

CHAPTER 1

INTRODUCTION

If you're holding this book, you're likely considering the idea of venturing into the world of vending machines —as a profitable side hustle or even a full-time business. The appeal is undeniable: low initial investment, low upkeep, and a source of revenue that doesn't demand your constant attention. Who wouldn't want to put their money into a company that appears to run itself?

But before you start ordering vending machines in bulk and looking for locations, let's take a step back. What might appear to be a *set-and-forget* business comes with its obstacles, opportunities, and expectations that you should be aware of.

Why this book is for you

This book's goal is not to discourage you but to provide a practical and actionable plan for getting into the vending machine business. You'll learn about every aspect of the vending machine industry from the ground up. We'll debunk myths and share case studies highlighting effective practices and common problems. You will study the art and science of turning vending machines into a viable, long-term business.

We'll explore issues such as:

- Choosing the correct type of vending machine for your target market

- Finding profitable locations and negotiating contracts
- Understanding the costs involved, including upfront and ongoing expenses
- Inventory management, upkeep, and replenishment
- Marketing strategies to make your vending machines stand out
- Scaling your business for long-term success and growth

1.1 The Myth of Passive Income

Chances are, you've come across a bunch of YouTube videos, blogs, or social media posts promoting vending machines as a source of "passive income." These posts sing praises of the many benefits of the vending business that come without putting in a lot of work.

Passive income has become a buzzword that sparks the interest of aspiring entrepreneurs, business students, and anyone trying to break free from the 9-to-5 grind. The concept seems simple: Set up a business model that requires minimal effort and watch the money roll in while you sleep, vacation, or focus on other ventures. It's a tempting idea, fueled by stories of people making six figures with little to no active involvement in their businesses.

Why Vending Machines Seem Like Easy Money

Vending machines are present in our everyday environment—from offices to schools to public transport stations— You're so used to them being around that you might not even see them when you walk by. Still, they are silently testifying that they are a viable business model.

It's easy to assume that someone is making a lot of money with minimal effort from these machines. But as we'll discuss in the following chapters, the reality has many more layers.

Many romanticize the notion of vending machine businesses. While they can be profitable, classifying them as "passive income" is a deceptive oversimplification. That's not to argue vending machines are a lousy investment; on the contrary, they're a great one. But before you get in headfirst, you must realize what you're getting into.

Setting up a vending machine business—or any business for that matter—requires substantial work, money, and, most importantly, time. Actual profit in the vending machine industry results from careful planning, persistent execution, and a determination to grow and adapt. It requires regularly analyzing your competition, knowing your consumers' needs, and especially striving for operational perfection. In a nutshell, it's far from 'passive.'

The Road to Profit: What It Truly Demands

So why, despite all these challenges, are we still talking about vending machine businesses? Because it *is* a viable business model when approached correctly. It's a business that can offer flexibility, growth opportunities, and, yes, profits. But like any business, it requires a well-thought-out strategy, a strong work ethic, and a willingness to adapt and grow.

In the upcoming chapters, we will dive deeper into each aspect of the vending machine business, from choosing your niche and securing your locations to managing your finances and scaling your operations.

This book is your guide to making real profit. By the time you finish, you'll be well-equipped to decide whether this business is right for you and how to make it a profitable venture.

1.2: The Time and Effort Required

While vending is not as demanding as some other business models, a vending machine operation does require a substantial commitment of time, effort, and financial resources.

If you're passionate about the business and willing to put in the hard work, there's certainly money to be made. Just don't go in expecting it to be a side gig that runs itself. Treat it as a real business, give it the attention it deserves, and you have a real shot at building a profitable venture. Let's take an overview of what is required.

Initial Setup: The Hidden Time Sink

Most newcomers underestimate the amount of time and energy required just to get started. Before your machine takes a single coin, you must go through an exhaustive process that includes:

- Market research to identify the most profitable locations.
- Negotiating contracts with property owners.
- Obtaining necessary licenses and permits.
- Purchasing the vending machine(s) and other equipment.
- Initial stocking and configuring of the machines.

This is no weekend project; it's a considerable commitment of your time and effort. Fail to give due diligence to any of these steps, and you're setting yourself up for problems down the line.

Continuous Stocking and Maintenance

The most underestimated and critical aspect of running a vending machine business is consistent stocking and regular maintenance. It's not merely a matter of refilling stock; it's a fundamental part of the operation that can significantly impact your cash flow and time management. Running out of popular items or having a non-functioning machine frustrates customers, eats into your profits, and tarnishes your reputation. Properly managing and forecasting your inventory needs and machine maintenance is imperative to sustain a successful vending business.

Financial Management: Not Just Counting Coins

Financial management in the vending machine business goes far beyond just counting coins and refilling stock. You need to keep track of sales patterns, restocking costs, machine wear and tear, and regular maintenance expenses. You must consider working capital for the change in your machines if you offer cash payment. Not to mention, you'll also have to deal with accounting, tax filing, and possibly payroll if you decide to employ someone to help you manage the machines.

Logistics: Not As Simple As A to B

Imagine your machine is at a location 20 miles away from your home, and you have to restock it every week. Even a slight delay due to traffic or other issues could throw your whole schedule off. The logistical complexities multiply if you have multiple machines scattered across different locations.

Time Commitment to Customer Service

Even though you are selling through a machine, customer service is still key. Dealing with stuck items, malfunctioning payment systems, and general inquiries are all part and parcel of running a vending machine business. Just because you don't have a physical store doesn't mean you can ignore customer complaints—ignoring them could result in a loss of contract, long-term customers, or even legal action.

Vending is also about providing a quality experience for the consumer. This means ensuring that the products are fresh, the machine is clean, and the user interface is intuitive. All these factors require regular checks and quality assurance measures that eat into your time and are often more complicated than they appear.

Scaling: More Machines can be More Problems

The idea of scaling the business—adding more vending machines— seems like the logical next step once you've got one machine turning a profit. But be warned: scaling doesn't simply mean replicating what you've done on a larger scale. Each new machine comes with its own set of challenges, including all the points listed above. And the time commitment isn't linear; managing ten machines will require more than ten times the effort of managing one.

Now that you have a clearer understanding of the basics of what goes into running a vending machine business, you can approach it with realistic expectations and a willingness to invest the necessary time and effort. Let's push forward.

CHAPTER 2

UNDERSTANDING VENDING MACHINES

Before diving into the nuts and bolts of launching a vending machine business, it's crucial to truly understand the machinery itself. Vending machines are more than just 'metal boxes that dispense snacks.' They are complex systems requiring operational, financial, and strategic understanding.

Types of Vending Machines

Vending machines come in various types:

- **Snack Machines:** These are the most common and dispensed items like chips, candy, and granola bars.
- **Drink Machines:** These specialize in cold beverages like soda, juice, and bottled water.
- **Combo Machines:** These offer both snacks and drinks (refrigerated).
- **Coffee Vending Machines:** Often found in offices, these machines dispense various kinds of coffee and other hot drinks.
- **Smart Vending Machines:** These regularly vend unique items like electronics, books, toys, or even freshly made foods. These machines boast advanced features, customizations, and

interactive interfaces, enhancing the user experience.

- **Bulk Vending Machines:** These machines typically dispense small, often low-cost items such as gumballs, toys, stickers, or even small snacks.

Your choice of machine type will heavily impact the location, target audience, and, potentially, the profitability of your venture.

2.1: What can I sell in my Vending Machines

When it comes to vending machines, one size does not fit all. Numerous solutions are available, each catering to a specific niche or serving a particular need. They require strategic thinking, careful planning, and especially a deep understanding of your consumer needs. The right type of vending machine can be the cornerstone of a profitable business, but the wrong choice can also set you back significantly.

So, first things first, you must decide what product you want to expend, and some products work better than others. Here's a comprehensive list of the most popular product types that can be sold through vending machines:

Traditional Snack and Beverage Vending Machines

These are the most common and well-known types of vending machines. The foundation of the vending machine industry is known for its widespread availability and popularity. They offer the basics: chips, candy bars, sodas, and juices. While not particularly glamorous, they are the bread and butter of the vending machine industry. These machines are commonly found in office buildings, schools, and transportation hubs. They may offer a 'quick fix' for hungry or thirsty consumers but rarely provide substantial meals. Here's a deeper look into this fundamental vending machine category:

Product Selection

- **Snacks:** Vending machines typically stock a range of snacks, including chips, pretzels, nuts, granola bars, and cookies. The variety appeals to diverse tastes and preferences.

- **Candy Bars:** A selection of popular candy bars attracts those with a sweet tooth, offering a quick energy boost or a delightful treat.
- **Beverages:** Common beverage options include sodas, bottled water, juices, sports drinks, and sometimes energy drinks.

Target Locations

Traditional snack and beverage vending machines are strategically placed in high-traffic locations such as office buildings, schools, hospitals, shopping centers, gyms, recreational facilities, and transportation hubs.

They cater to busy individuals seeking a convenient and accessible source of sustenance or a quick snack during their daily routines.

Consumer Convenience

The primary advantage of these machines lies in their accessibility and ease of use. Consumers can quickly satisfy their cravings or thirst by inserting money or using cashless payment options, making it a hassle-free experience.

They offer a 'grab-and-go' convenience, saving time for individuals with tight schedules or those in need of a quick snack between activities.

Product Rotation and Freshness

Maintaining product freshness is vital to retain customer satisfaction.

Vending operators need to implement effective product rotation and restocking strategies to ensure that items are within their shelf life, typically ranging from a few weeks to a few months, depending on the product type.

Profit Margins

The traditional snack and beverage vending machine model often provides a stable source of revenue with relatively consistent profit margins. Operators need to carefully balance pricing to remain competitive and profitable in the market. On average, the profit margin for snacks and beverages in vending machines ranges from 30% to 50%, varying based on product pricing, location, and operational costs.

Technology Integration

Modern vending machines are increasingly integrating technology for improved functionality. This includes features like cashless payment systems, real-time inventory monitoring, and data analytics to optimize product offerings based on consumer preferences.

Coffee Machines

Coffee vending machines have gained immense popularity in recent years, catering to the ever-growing demand for a quick caffeine fix among busy individuals. These machines offer a range of coffee options, from classic black coffee to specialty lattes and cappuccinos. Here are some key points to consider about coffee vending machines:

Types of Coffee Machines

- **Traditional Coffee Machines:** These machines provide standard coffee options like black coffee, espresso, and Americano. They are cost-effective and well-suited for locations with a high demand for simple coffee choices.
- **Bean-to-Cup Machines:** These machines grind coffee beans on the spot, ensuring a fresher cup of coffee. They offer a variety of coffee styles and can replicate the taste of a coffee shop.

Target Audience

Coffee vending machines primarily target office buildings, bus and train stations, and hospitals, where people often seek a quick and convenient coffee option. On-the-go professionals especially appreciate the efficiency and speed of coffee vending machines.

Customization and Options

Many coffee vending machines allow customization of coffee strength, size, and sweetness levels to cater to individual preferences.

Some advanced machines even offer dairy alternatives like almond or soy milk, appealing to a broader customer base, including those with dietary restrictions.

Maintenance and Quality Control:

Maintenance is crucial for coffee machines to deliver a high-quality cup of coffee consistently.

Regular cleaning and maintenance schedules should be in place to keep the machines in optimal working condition and maintain the taste and hygiene of the coffee. It's especially vital to pay attention to the tubing system to prevent any hindrance in the coffee-making process.

Specialized Food and Drink Machines

From gourmet coffee dispensers to machines that sell freshly squeezed orange juice, specialized food and drink vending machines aim to offer something more unique than the regular snack machine. They can be an excellent choice for areas with high foot traffic and a demographic willing to pay a premium for quality and convenience.

Specialized food and drink vending machines represent a niche within the industry, offering distinctive and higher-quality food and beverage options beyond the typical snacks and drinks. These machines cater to consumers seeking a premium and unique vending experience. Here's an in-depth exploration of this specialized category:

Product Selection

- **Gourmet Coffee Machines:** These machines serve high-quality coffee options, often utilizing freshly ground beans and providing a variety of coffee styles such as lattes, cappuccinos, and espressos.
- **Freshly Squeezed Juice Machines:** These machines provide

health-conscious consumers with a healthy and refreshing beverage option.

- **Salad and Healthy Meal Machines:** Some vending machines now offer salads, wraps, and other healthy meal options, appealing to those looking for nutritious and convenient food choices.
- **Frozen Yogurt or Ice Cream Machines:** These machines dispense frozen treats like frozen yogurt or ice cream, offering a delightful dessert or snack option.

Target Audience and Locations

Specialized food and drink vending machines are strategically placed in areas with high foot traffic and a demographic willing to pay a premium for quality and convenience.

Fresh food vending machines target health-conscious individuals seeking convenient and wholesome food options that align with their dietary preferences and wellness goals.

Locations with health-focused demographics, such as upscale office complexes, health and fitness centers, hospitals, shopping malls, and premium entertainment venues, are ideal spots for these machines.

Premium Pricing and Perceived Value

Products from specialized vending machines often come at a higher price point than regular vending items, reflecting the quality and uniqueness of the offerings.

Consumers are willing to pay more for the premium experience and the perception of higher quality associated with specialized vending options.

Maintenance and Quality Assurance

Maintaining the quality of specialized food and drink vending machines is paramount to upholding the premium image. Regular cleaning, servicing, and ensuring product freshness are essential for customer satisfaction.

Operators must carefully manage inventory to prevent spoilage, particularly with perishable items like fresh juices or salads.

Operators must carefully monitor expiration dates, promptly remove expired items, and restock fresh products to ensure customer satisfaction and compliance with food safety regulations.

Technological Advancements

Specialized vending machines often incorporate advanced technologies such as touchscreens for easy selection, customization features, and smart inventory management systems to optimize restocking and reduce downtime.

Food Safety Compliance

Adhering to stringent food safety standards and guidelines is crucial for fresh food vending machines to ensure the safety and well-being of consumers.

Proper temperature control, hygiene, and storage practices are vital to maintaining food safety and minimizing health risks.

Office Supply Vending Machines

The traditional nine-to-five workday confined within office walls has evolved into a more flexible model. Many individuals now split their work hours between home and office, and ensuring access to necessary tools and supplies has become crucial. Office supply vending machines are lifesavers in corporate settings. Placed strategically within an office or near a coworking space, they offer a convenient way for people to access essential supplies without leaving the premises. The trick here is to stock useful and often forgotten or lost items.

Product Selection

Office supply vending machines stock a variety of items essential for productivity in a work environment. This can include pens, notepads, USB drives, headphones, charging cables, and even small office gadgets.

The selection is carefully curated to include frequently needed items, often forgotten or required in urgent situations.

Location Strategy

These vending machines are strategically placed within corporate offices, coworking spaces, business centers, and university campuses, targeting locations where individuals may require office supplies at any given time.

High-traffic areas like lobbies, near meeting rooms, or communal workspaces are ideal spots for these machines.

Tracking and Restocking

Advanced vending machines are equipped with technology that allows real-time tracking of inventory levels. This data helps operators manage restocking efficiently and ensures the machines are consistently well-supplied.

Personal Care Vending Machines

These vending machines sell personal care items like toothpaste, deodorant, feminine hygiene products, and even small pharmacy items like over-the-counter medicines. You'll often find these machines in restrooms at airports or event venues. For these machines to be profitable, they must be located where people will need these items in a pinch.

Product selection

Personal care vending machines provide a range of items such as toothpaste, toothbrushes, deodorants, feminine hygiene products, pain relievers, band-aids, and other over-the-counter medicines.

The selection caters to immediate needs and common personal care emergencies.

Ideal Locations

Personal care vending machines are strategically placed in restrooms, near entrances, or in areas with high foot traffic, ensuring accessibility to people in need of personal care items in a pinch.

Locations like airports, bus or train stations, and event venues, as well as hotels and motels, are popular spots for these vending machines.

Emergency Convenience

The primary advantage of personal care vending machines is their convenience during unexpected situations, such as forgetting a toothbrush while traveling or needing a pain reliever urgently. Providing a 24/7 solution where there is constant foot traffic and limited alternatives can be an unmatched convenience, making them a valuable asset in high-traffic locations like airports.

Automated Retail Vending Machines

Imagine buying electronics, toys, or even clothing from a vending machine. That's what automated retail vending machines offer—a self-service shopping experience for a wide range of products. These are sophisticated machines often integrated with touchscreens and various payment options, including mobile payment systems. They are usually located in high-traffic areas and require a significant investment.

The best way to envision an automated vending machine is not merely as a vending machine with better features but as a fully automated, self-attending store.

Product Selection

Automated retail vending machines offer a diverse range of products, including electronics (chargers, headphones), toys, clothing accessories, beauty products, and even small to medium-sized gadgets or electronics.

The product range is carefully curated to appeal to the target audience and align with the location's demographic.

Technological Integration

These vending machines are equipped with advanced technology, including touchscreen interfaces that provide detailed product information and enable smooth navigation.

Multiple payment options, such as credit cards, mobile payment systems, and cash, are integrated to enhance user convenience and accommodate varying preferences.

Location Strategy

Automated retail vending machines are strategically placed in high-traffic areas like shopping malls, airports, train stations, and busy urban centers.

The locations are chosen to ensure maximum visibility and

accessibility, attracting potential customers seeking a quick shopping solution.

Investment and Profitability

Establishing automated retail vending machines requires a significant initial investment due to the technology involved and the need for a diverse product inventory.

Profitability is often driven by the higher price points of the products sold, compensating for the initial investment and operational costs.

Bulk Vending Machines

You often see these smaller vending machines in grocery stores near the exit. They dispense small toys, candy, or even stickers. Because of their low price point and smaller size, they're a popular choice for entrepreneurs just starting in the vending machine business. However, these machines often require more frequent restocking and might offer lower profit margins.

Product Selection

Bulk vending machines offer a selection of small, low-cost items, making them appealing to a wide range of customers, especially children and bargain seekers.

Typical items include small toys, gumballs, temporary tattoos, stickers, and novelty trinkets.

Restocking and Profit Margins

Bulk vending machines often require frequent restocking due to the items' small size and popularity.

Profit margins may be lower compared to other vending machines, but the volume of sales often compensates for this, making them a profitable venture.

Target Locations

Bulk vending machines are typically placed in family-oriented locations like grocery stores, malls, arcades, amusement parks, and restaurants, where they can attract children and families.

CHAPTER 3

BUSINESS PLANNING

A business plan isn't a mere formality for investors—it's a concrete strategy defining your business's trajectory. It outlines your mission, vision, goals, and steps to achieve them. For a vending machine business, it's your plan for location scouting, supplier contracts, maintenance, and contingency plans.

Key Elements of a Vending Machine Business Plan

Let's start by understanding the fundamental elements that should go into your business plan:

1. **Executive Summary:** A concise overview of your business and why it will succeed.
2. **Business Description:** A more detailed explanation of your business, the problem it solves, and why it's unique.
3. **Market Research:** In-depth analysis of your target market, competition, and demand for vending machine services.
4. **Business Structure:** Details on whether you operate as a sole proprietor, a partnership, or an LLC.
5. **Product Line:** Details about the products and services you will offer, in this case, mainly the items you'll sell through your vending machines.
6. **Marketing and Sales Strategy:** How you plan to attract

customers and keep them coming back.

7. **Operations Plan:** The logistics of obtaining and maintaining your vending machines, stocking products, and general upkeep.

8. **Financial Projections:** A look at your funding requirements, projected income, expenses, and profitability. Try and imagine the next five years.

Building the Business Plan

1. Executive Summary

Your executive summary should give a snapshot of what your vending machine business aims to do and how you plan to do it. If you're seeking external funding, this section should be compelling enough to catch an investor's interest. While it's the first part of your plan, it's often easier to write it last when you have a clearer picture of your comprehensive strategy.

2. Business Description

Describe the niche you're planning to fill. Is there a lack of vending machines in a particular location? Do existing machines not offer what the local demographic desires? This is your chance to state why your business matters. It should be crisp, focused, and packed with essential information.

This section offers the opportunity to outline your business model. Are you focusing on healthy snacks or targeting busy office buildings with traditional offerings? Discuss the state of the industry and how your business fits into the larger picture.

3. Market Research

Identify and understand your target audience—Are you aiming for corporate offices, schools, or shopping malls? Each of these options presents a unique set of challenges and opportunities. You should also look at the existing competition—direct (other vending machines) and indirect (cafeterias, convenience stores).

Your Market Analysis should be comprehensive and data-driven. Who is your target customer? What locations offer the best prospects? Are there seasonal trends you should be aware of?

4. Business Structure

Deciding on your business structure is crucial for tax purposes, liability, and ownership control. Consult a business advisor or legal expert to determine what works best for you. Whether a sole proprietorship or an LLC, each structure has its own set of advantages and disadvantages.

Choosing the proper business structure is important for tax optimization, liability protection, and ownership control. Seek guidance from a business advisor or legal expert to tailor the structure that suits your specific needs. Whether a sole proprietorship or an LLC, each option has distinct advantages and drawbacks. Anticipate future possibilities—such as adding a partner or selling your business—and plan your structure accordingly. Thinking ahead ensures your business structure remains adaptable to your evolving needs and aspirations.

5. Product Line

Detail the vending machines you'll be using and what products you'll offer. Will you sell snacks, beverages, and non-traditional products such as electronics or office supplies? Consider the shelf-life, demand, and profitability of each item. The product mix could make or break your venture.

6. Marketing and Sales Strategy

You need to outline how you plan to attract customers. Remember, the placement of your vending machines and how they look and communicate is a form of marketing, too. Importantly, have a retention strategy; happy customers who come back are often more valuable than attracting new ones.

7. Operations Plan

This section should detail the day-to-day management of your vending machine business. Everything needs to be documented, from sourcing and installing machines to restocking and maintenance. Be explicit about the tasks you plan to handle versus those that might require third-party services, and note how much they will cost.

8. Financial Projections

Calculate your initial setup costs, monthly expenses, and expected revenue. Be realistic with your estimates and try to anticipate unplanned costs. Financial projections give you a metric by which you can gauge the success of your venture. Clearly identify how much you'll need to start and how much you'll need to keep the business running.

It's a good practice to provide a financial forecast for the next five years, including profit and loss projections, cash flow forecasts, and balance sheets.

Iterate, Iterate, Iterate!

Keep in mind a business plan is not set in stone. As your business evolves, so should your plan. Consistently review and update it to reflect current realities, especially if you're pivoting your business model or entering new markets. The more accurately your plan mirrors your business, the more valuable it will be as a tool for success.

Throughout this book, we'll expand on each of the above business plan elements. With all these aspects carefully outlined, you won't merely perceive the vending machine business as a 'passive income' alternative. Instead, you'll have the insights and plans needed to make it a profitable and fulfilling business.

CHAPTER 4

MARKET RESEARCH & LOCATION

Choosing the right spots for your vending machines is a strategic game-changer. In this chapter, we break down how savvy market research and keen consumer insights steer you toward optimal locations, boosting your vending business's success. Don't underestimate this game-changing step.

Why Market Research Matters

Yes, even in the seemingly straightforward business of vending machines, market research is vital. The success of your vending machine operation is hugely dependent on where the machine is located, what it sells, and who will be walking by it.

Market research helps you answer these questions so you can better tailor your product offerings and identify ideal locations. This information is crucial not just for maximizing sales but also for differentiating your vending machine in a crowded market.

The Basics: Demographics and Psychographics

Begin by asking who your potential customers are. Are they high school students, office workers, or gym-goers? Research the demographics and psychographics of these groups. Understanding their age, income level, and lifestyle choices can guide your product selection and pricing. It's crucial to really observe what's going on, take your time, and ask around, but don't just take someone's word for it.

For instance, if you install a vending machine for office workers, the HR department will surely ask you for health-conscious options, possibly organic snacks and bottled water. However, more often than not, what the workers are really craving are quick sodas and some candy. Understanding your target audience's preferences is key to effectively tailoring your offerings.

Understanding the Area

Scout the geographical locations you are considering. You'll want to know:

- **Foot Traffic:** High foot traffic is vital, but the quality of that traffic matters more than sheer quantity—target areas with foot traffic relevant to your product. For example, placing a vending machine next to an ATM might attract a different demographic compared to placing it in a high-traffic area where individuals are hurriedly rushing home after a long day.
- **Accessibility:** Ensure the location is easily accessible to your target audience. A location with high foot traffic but poor accessibility won't benefit your business.
- **Competition:** Assess nearby competition. Placing a vending machine next to a similar business can lead to direct competition. Choose locations where your offerings stand out

and cater to unmet needs. A vending machine near a convenience store rarely sells well.

- **Security:** Prioritize safety. A secure location not only protects your investment but also ensures customer confidence. Vandalism or break-ins can severely impact your business operations and reputation.

Strategic Locations

Below are some of the usual subjects of strategic locations for vending machines to consider:

Schools and Colleges

- **Insights:** High Foot Traffic: Educational institutions experience a constant flow of students, faculty, and staff throughout the day.
- **Health and Wellness Guidelines:** Given the increasing focus on health, offering nutritious snacks in compliance with school guidelines is crucial.

Offices

- **Insights:** Recurring Monthly Quotas: Collaborate with offices to establish a monthly quota of products, providing a secured monthly income and creating a reliable customer base.
- **Employee Preferences:** Tailor your vending selection based on employees' preferences, often in need of a quick snack or a caffeine boost during their workday.

Hospitals

- **Insights:** 24/7 Foot Traffic: Hospitals have a continuous influx of foot traffic around the clock, catering to a diverse audience, including patients, visitors, and healthcare providers.
- **Diverse Dietary Needs:** Accommodate a range of dietary needs due to patients and staff with varying nutritional requirements.

Public Transit Hubs

- **Insights:** Impulsive Purchases: Individuals waiting for their next bus or train often make impulsive purchases. Choose locations where foot traffic naturally pauses without causing congestion and avoid areas where people are rushing.
- **Variety and Convenience:** Offer the hurried commuter a variety of quick, on-the-go snacks and beverages. Also, consider non-traditional vending products (earphones, books, electronics).

Gyms

- **Insights:** Gyms attract health-conscious individuals, making stocking up on healthy snacks and nutritional supplements ideal.
- **Partnerships and Promotions:** Explore partnerships with gyms where the vending service could be offered without direct charges, enhancing customer engagement and service accessibility.

Testing the Waters

If possible, consider a soft launch. Place your vending machine for a limited period and monitor sales. This will provide valuable insights into customer behavior and preferences, allowing you to fine-tune your strategy.

Constantly Update

Consumer preferences change, new competitors emerge, and things happen that make locations lose their appeal. Keep an eye on your sales data, customer feedback, and market trends to constantly fine-tune your strategy. When setting up the contract, it's also a good idea to give flexibility, when possible, to the agreed location, just in case it doesn't sell as expected.

4.1: Competition Analysis

Like any business, understanding your market and especially your competition is key. But how do you analyze your competitors in a vending machine business? Competition analysis isn't about imitation but differentiation. Knowing what others are doing can help you carve out your unique value proposition. What sets your vending machines apart? Is it the product, the location, or perhaps an innovative payment system? Only by studying your competitors can you answer these questions effectively.

The Layers of Competition

Competition isn't just the vending machine next to yours. It's more layered than that:

- **Direct Competition**: These are other vending machine businesses that sell similar products, likely targeting the same audience. Direct competitors are often the most visible and concerning layer of competition.
- **Indirect Competition**: These could be convenience stores, cafeterias, or other outlets that offer a similar range of products as your vending machine but aren't vending machines themselves.
- **Substitute Competition**: What are your potential customers doing if you have no direct or indirect competitors at the location? Are they finding a substitute for what you want to offer?

A practical rule of thumb that might seem obvious is to target locations where your vending machine possesses a clear advantage, so much so that it faces little to no competition. This could mean opting for spots with 24/7-foot traffic, where conventional stores can't maintain a constant presence. Or consider locations that uniquely suit your offering and only machines can fit, such as installing a cigarette vending machine in a bustling casino.

Steps to Analyze Competition

1. **Identify Your Competitors**: First, make a list. It's not just about knowing who they are but understanding what they offer and how they operate. Do some footwork. Visit the location and identify the type of competitors. Note the products they offer, their pricing, their best-selling products, and any unique features or promotions they might be running.

2. **Analyze Strengths and Weaknesses**: Each competitor will have certain advantages and disadvantages. Perhaps one competing vending machine has a prime location but outdated machines. The convenience store might offer a variety of products but has high prices. Take note of these.

3. **Customer Feedback**: Your competitors' users can offer insights you can't get elsewhere. Observe, or if possible, chat with people in your desired location. Find out what they like or dislike, especially what's missing.

4. **Market Trends**: The industry is always subject to trends. Organic or health-focused snacks, touchless payments, etc., are all trends you should be aware of.

Turning Information into Strategy

Once you've gathered all this data, it's time to turn it into a strategy. Determine the gaps in your competitors' strategies and think about how you can fill them. Identify your advantage.

Unique Value Proposition (UVP)

Define a clear Unique Value Proposition (UVP) based on your analysis. How will your vending machine business stand out in a crowded market? Highlight what makes your offerings unique and why customers should choose your machines over competitors.

SWOT Analysis

Do a SWOT (Strengths, Weaknesses, Opportunities, Threats) analysis based on the data gathered. This structured assessment will help you identify internal strengths and weaknesses and external opportunities and threats, guiding your strategy formulation.

Pricing and Product Strategy

Develop a pricing and product strategy that capitalizes on your identified advantages. Determine the optimal pricing for your products that balances competitiveness and profitability. Additionally, plan your product range based on the gaps you identified.

Operational Efficiencies

Explore how you can streamline your operations based on the weaknesses you observed in your competitors. Can you optimize routes, improve maintenance efficiency, or enhance customer service? Operational efficiencies can translate to cost savings and improved customer experiences.

CHAPTER 5

LEGAL & REGULATORY CONSIDERATIONS

You've assessed the market, understood your audience, got a location, and even identified the ideal vending machines for your new business. Great! But don't hit that 'purchase' button just yet. Before you jump in, there are some critical legal and regulatory considerations to navigate.

5.1 Licensing and Permits

Your vending machine operation will require specific licenses and permits. Each country and city has its own requirements, so it's essential to check local laws and regulations. Here are some common ones you might need:

Types of Permits and Licenses

1. **General Business License:** Before you do anything else, you'll need a general business license. This is an essential requirement for any business, and it's usually issued by the city where you plan to operate. The cost varies widely from jurisdiction to jurisdiction, but expect to pay between $50 and $400.

2. **Vending Machine License:** This is the big one. The license is often per machine and can cost anywhere from $25 to $200

per machine per year, depending on your location.

3. **Food Handling Permit:** If you plan to vend perishable items like sandwiches, salads, or any type of fresh food, you might need a food handling permit. Depending on the specifics, these can range from $100 to $1,000.

4. **Location Permits:** Some public and private locations require additional permits. Malls, schools, and corporate campuses often have their own rules, which may involve additional costs.

5. **State-Specific Licenses:** Some states have unique requirements that might require additional fees. For example, California has a specific "Vending Machine Food License" that could add another layer of costs.

The Application Process

Applying for permits and licenses involves paperwork, possibly some inspections, and, of course, fees. You'll likely have to provide detailed business information, tax ID numbers, and maybe even a business plan. The complexity of this process varies depending on where you are, but expect it to take several weeks or even months. Plan ahead.

Hidden Costs

Time is money, and the time you spend filling out applications and gathering documentation is time you're not spending on other areas of your business. Plus, it's very possible you need to hire legal or professional help to make sure you're filling everything out correctly. All this adds to your costs, and although it's hard to put an exact amount on these, remember to allocate a budget for legal fees and consultations to avoid any unexpected financial strain starting up and during your operation.

Renewals and Updates

Almost all permits and licenses require regular renewal, and yes, that means paying those fees again. Also, be prepared for occasional inspections and updated regulations that might require you to apply for new permits.

Penalties for Non-Compliance

Fines for non-compliance can range from a few hundred dollars to thousands, depending on the infringement. Worse, you may also face temporary business closure. The short-term cost savings of dodging these fees are not worth the long-term risks.

5.2 Insurance: Protecting the Business

Compliance with legal and insurance requirements is more than a prudent business practice; it's often a legal necessity based on your country and where your machines are located. Make sure you're in the know and comply with these rules.

Liability Insurance

Liability insurance helps you protect your vending machine business from potential financial losses arising from accidents, injuries, or damages related to your vending machines. Depending on your region, this insurance may be a legal requirement. It's prudent to consult with a reputable insurance provider to understand the specific coverage options available for vending machine businesses and ensure your venture is adequately protected. Even if it's not a requirement based on your location and the type of product you are selling, it usually is highly advisable. Just envision the financial implications of a coffee burn, and the importance becomes crystal clear.

Covering Your Machines and Operations

As for insurance for your machine and operation, you must seek policies that address product liability, equipment breakdown, theft, and, if possible, business interruption. It's essential to assess your operational risks and consult with insurance professionals to tailor a coverage package that effectively fortifies your vending machine venture. As vending machine insurance isn't standard, prices can vary significantly, and it's essential to compare several options to secure the best deal.

5.3: Health and Safety Regulations

Vending machines are part of the food and retail industry, offering products that people consume or use. This comes with a duty of care towards the consumers. Just like restaurants must maintain kitchen hygiene, depending on your location and what you sell, vending machine operators legally must ensure their machines are sanitary, functional, and safe to use.

FDA Regulations

The Food and Drug Administration (FDA) plays a crucial role in regulating vending machines, particularly those that dispense food and beverages in the United States. If your vending machine sells perishable items such as sandwiches, dairy products, or even some types of snacks, you are obligated to follow FDA guidelines.

- **Temperature Control:** The vending machine must have a mechanism to maintain the right temperature for perishable items.
- **Labeling:** Proper labels, including ingredients, nutritional facts, and expiration dates, should be displayed.
- **Sanitation:** Regular cleaning schedules should be maintained.

Some other countries have similar regulations, and some emerging markets are more permissive, but sooner than later, regulations will arrive, and even if not currently enforced rigorously, it's always good to do everything you can to prevent any health hazards in the future.

State and Local Laws

Besides federal laws, you'll also need to pay attention to state and local regulations. These laws may vary significantly and include additional stipulations, such as health permits or operating licenses. Always consult with a local attorney who is familiar with the vending machine laws in your area to ensure you are in compliance.

Inspections

It's uncommon, but don't be surprised if you are subjected to random inspections by health departments or other regulatory bodies. These inspections ensure you maintain the vending machines according to the required standards. Failure to pass these inspections could result in warnings, fines, or even your business's temporary or permanent closure.

Accessibility and Safety

In the United States, the Americans with Disabilities Act (ADA) specifies the requirements for vending machine accessibility. Similarly, electrical and mechanical safety standards must be adhered to, ensuring that the machines pose no danger to the users.

Documentation and Record-Keeping

Keep meticulous records of machine maintenance, inspections, permits, and any communications with regulatory bodies. Good record-keeping not only makes it easier to prove compliance but also to manage the business more efficiently.

5.4: The Rest of the Legal Landscape

Other crucial legal aspects demand your attention beyond permits, insurance, and health regulations. Let's explore these key considerations:

Employment Laws

If your business grows to the point where you need to hire employees—for restocking, maintenance, or administration—you'll need to be aware of employment laws. This includes minimum wage, employee benefits, working conditions, and other legal obligations as an employer.

Location and Zoning Laws

While vending machines can technically go anywhere, you can't just place them willy-nilly. Zoning laws dictate the kinds of businesses that can operate in specific areas. Even if a property owner gives you the go-ahead, you still need to make sure the zoning laws allow for vending operations.

Retailer Agreements

A retailer or site agreement is required if you plan to place your vending machine in someone else's facility, such as a gym, school, or office building. This legally binding contract details the conditions of your agreement, such as any rent or commissions due to the property owner, maintenance schedules, and other responsibilities.

Contracts with Suppliers

Your vending machine needs to be stocked, which means you'll need a steady supply of items to sell. Often, you'll have to enter into contracts with suppliers, and each contract will come with its own set of obligations, payment terms, and legal requirements. We'll discuss supplier relationships in detail in Chapter 7, extending this strategic understanding in the upcoming discussion.

Tax Considerations

Taxes are an inescapable facet of any business; your vending machine operation is no exception. Rigorous record-keeping of sales, expenses, employee wages, and more is essential. Depending on your jurisdiction, you may encounter income tax and sales tax.

CHAPTER 6

PURCHASING &
MAINTAINING MACHINES

Buying a vending machine is about more than just having the cash upfront. It's a decision that constantly affects your business's cash flow. Initially, all machines might seem similar, but down the line, they require maintenance, repairs, and parts—costs that can eat into your cash flow. A machine out of order isn't just a minor inconvenience; it's a direct hit on your finances. In this chapter, we dive into this crucial decision, guiding you on balancing the upfront cost with the ongoing financial health of your vending machine business.

6.1 Choosing the Right Vending Machines

Picking the right vending machine is more than just choosing the most affordable option or the one with the best aesthetics. Several factors should influence your choice:

- **Type of Products:** The type of products you plan to sell will dictate the machine you need. Snack items and beverages, for example, have different storage and dispensing requirements.
- **Location Requirements:** Is your location indoor or outdoor?
- **Payment Options:** Modern vending machines offer various payment options, including cash, cards, and mobile payments. Make sure your machine is equipped with the payment

methods popular in your target location.

- **Energy Efficiency:** An eco-friendly decision if you can afford it. Also, depending on your location, a more energy-efficient machine could save you money on your monthly bill.

6.2: Buying vs. Leasing

Each option comes with its own set of advantages and drawbacks, and understanding these can significantly impact the financial health and long-term trajectory of your vending business.

Buying Vending Machines

When you opt for ownership, the advantages include having complete control over the machine—modify, relocate, or sell it as needed—along with the absence of recurring payments offering financial relief during slow business periods. Tax benefits in the form of depreciation add to its appeal, and the flexibility to operate without being bound by a contract is a notable advantage. However, this path also involves high upfront costs, which are potentially challenging for startups. Maintenance becomes your responsibility both in terms of time and costs. Additionally, given the rapid evolution of technology, your new machine may become obsolete sooner than expected.

Leasing Vending Machines

On the other hand, choosing to lease vending machines brings its own set of advantages. Leasing offers lower upfront costs, making starting your business easier without a substantial initial investment. Leasing companies often provide up-to-date equipment, ensuring you remain competitive regarding features and payment options. Maintenance support is typically included in leasing contracts, sparing you the hassle of dealing with mechanical issues. The flexibility of terms allows for upgrades or machine switches in alignment with your evolving business needs. However, this path accrues long-term costs that, over time, can surpass the actual cost of the machine. You won't own the machine at the end of the lease term, and any equity built through payments is forfeited unless you choose to purchase the machine. Lease agreements also come with contractual obligations, potentially limiting your operational flexibility.

6.3 New vs. Used Machines

If you decide to buy, which is the most common approach, you'll face the decision of whether to buy new or used vending machines. Each option has clear pros and cons.

New Machines:

Pros

- **Warranty:** Buying a new machine usually comes with a warranty, providing a safety net against potential malfunctions.
- **Reliability:** New machines are less likely to malfunction, especially refrigerated ones, ensuring consistent and reliable service for your customers.
- **Modern Features:** New vending machines often boast modern features, enhancing the overall user experience and operational efficiency.

Cons

- **Higher Upfront Cost:** The main drawback of new machines is the significant upfront investment required.

Used Machines:

Pros

- **Cost-Effective:** Opting for used machines involves a lower initial investment, making it a cost-effective choice, especially for testing locations or startups with budget constraints.

Cons

- **Potential for Malfunctions:** Used machines are more likely to malfunction due to wear and tear, potentially requiring more frequent maintenance.

Used vending machines tend to be significantly cheaper than their new counterparts, often ranging from 30% to 50% less in price. As a general recommendation for most, going for used vending machines would be the top choice based on practicality and cost-efficiency. They provide a smart entry point into the vending machine business, allowing you to test your business concept and location choices without a hefty initial investment. However, the choice ultimately depends on your comprehensive business plan and budget, so weigh the options and choose what best suits your unique circumstances.

6.4: Machine Maintenance

You've decided to buy or lease your vending machines and secured a great high-traffic location. Great! But, as we've stated quite a bit during this book, those machines aren't going to take care of themselves. Machine maintenance is not just an essential chore; it's an ongoing commitment that can make or break your venture.

Why Maintenance Matters

Imagine walking up to a vending machine, inserting your money, and then—nothing. No product, no change, just a sense of frustration. Not only have you lost a sale, but that dissatisfied customer is unlikely to risk their money again. Even worse, they'll likely share their bad experience with others. Regular maintenance is not just about keeping your machines running; it's about building and maintaining customer trust.

Types of Maintenance

- **Preventive Maintenance:** Regularly scheduled checks to ensure that machines are clean, fully functional, and well-stocked.
- **Corrective Maintenance:** Unscheduled repairs are carried out when a machine is faulty or broken.
- **Cosmetic Maintenance:** Cleaning and tidying up the machine and surrounding area, including refilling stock.

Who Should Do the Maintenance?

You've got a range of options to manage machine maintenance. Starting by handling it yourself is a <u>must</u> —it saves costs and provides essential insights into your business dynamics. Understanding how your machine operates, what sells well, and identifying issues is best experienced firsthand. There's no substitute for this direct involvement in grasping your business.

However, as your business scales, doing it alone becomes less practical. Delegating maintenance tasks is essential. You might opt to hire dedicated staff for this purpose. Alternatively, outsourcing is another route. Many specialized companies handle vending machine maintenance. While it can be less hassle and even cost-effective, ensure you're comfortable entrusting someone else with the care of your machines.

Preventive Maintenance Checklist

Consistency is key here; a good starting point is to create a checklist. Just as an example, here are some items that should be on that list for every visit to your vending machine:

- Clean glass fronts and keypads.
- Inspect for any physical damages.
- Run a software diagnostic (if available).
- Check coin and note acceptors for jam.
- Test machine for functionality.
- Check product expiry dates (if applicable).
- Restock products.
- Collect cash.

Tools and Supplies for Maintenance

Equipping yourself with the right tools and supplies is crucial for addressing common maintenance issues. Here's a simple yet comprehensive toolkit checklist as a starting point to keep things running smoothly:

- Multi-screwdriver set
- Cleaning supplies (cloths, sponges, all-purpose cleaners, paper towels, etc.)

- Lubricant for moving parts
- Spare change for the coin mechanism (If you accept cash – and if you have access to real-time data on the change in the machine, you'll be able to visit with the exact amount needed.)
- Spare parts (like replacement motors or coils)

Corrective Maintenance: Handling Breakdowns

When a machine breaks down, time is of the essence. The longer your machine is out of order, the more revenue you lose. The following are the most common issues, accounting for about 90% of breakdowns, along with troubleshooting steps:

- **Machine Not Powering On:** Start with the basics. Ensure the machine is properly plugged in and check the circuit breaker. If these are in order and the machine still won't power up, seeking professional assistance is advisable.
- **Payment device issue:** If the bill or coin device is causing problems, it could be due to dirt or a bill/coin jam. Carefully inspect and clean the device, ensuring it's lubricated if needed. Test with various bills and coins to confirm its functionality.
- **Product Not Dispensing:** If products aren't dispensing, check for jams in the product coils. Inspect the motor for signs of wear and replace if necessary to ensure proper dispensing. Also, check connectors to ensure they haven't loosened during restocking, which could disrupt the dispensing mechanism.

Here are a few more typical additional issues, depending on what type of machine you have:

- **Temperature Irregularities (For Refrigerated Machines):** If a vending machine has a refrigeration unit and you notice temperature irregularities, ensure the vents and coils are clean and not obstructed. Check the thermostat settings and adjust if needed.
- **Network or Connectivity Issues:** In modern vending machines that are connected to networks for inventory monitoring and transactions, connectivity problems are pretty common. Verify the network cables, Wi-Fi connections, or cellular signal strength. A simple reboot will usually resolve the issue.

Keeping a Maintenance Log

A maintenance log can be incredibly handy for tracking recurring issues, keeping up with cleaning schedules, and generally providing data that can help you make informed decisions about your machines. There is specialized software available, but a simple printed checklist per day is just fine to start with. The key is to have a systematic record of maintenance activities, making it easier to identify patterns, address recurring problems, and plan proactive maintenance.

Manual Maintenance Log Template

Here is a simple example of what your everyday vending machine maintenance log could look like:

Machine ID/Name: _____

Location: _____

Date: _____

Maintenance Activity	Notes/Comments
Machine Cleaning	[Enter details about the cleaning process.]
Physical damages	[Note any damages found during the inspection.]
Software diagnostic (if available)	[Describe the results of the software diagnostic.]
Coin and note acceptors jams	[Indicate if any jams were found and actions taken.]
Overall machine functionality	[Detail the results of the functionality test.]
Product expiry dates (if applicable)	[Note any expired products and actions taken.]
Restocked Products	[List the products restocked and quantities.]
Cash Collection	[Record the amount of cash collected.]
Additional Notes	[Enter any additional notes or observations related to maintenance.]

6.5: Always, always Budget in Repairs

We will be repeating this a few times throughout this book. You might think your primary costs for running a vending machine business are purchasing or leasing the machines and stocking them with goods. While that's partially true, an often-overlooked cost can sneak up on you: repairs.

Why Repairs Are Inevitable

Your vending machine is a mechanical and electrical device that will eventually require repairs. It could be due to wear and tear, accidental damage, or even vandalism. Whatever the cause, neglecting to account for repair costs in your budget could mean the difference between a profitable business and a struggling one.

Types of Repairs

- **Minor Repairs:** These are simple issues like jammed coins, stuck items, or replacing a burned-out light bulb.
- **Major Repairs:** These include replacing motors, fixing electrical problems, or dealing with structural issues.
- **Emergency Repairs:** These are unexpected and urgent issues that require immediate attention to keep the machine operational.

Costs Associated with Repairs

While it's hard to pinpoint the exact cost for each type of repair, here are some rough estimates:

- Minor Repairs: $20 - $50
- Major Repairs: $100 - $500
- Emergency Repairs: $100 - $700

Note: These are just rough figures and can vary depending on your machine's make model and the severity of the issue.

Setting Up a Repair Budget

When it comes to budgeting for repairs, there are a few strategies you can adopt:

- **Fixed Monthly Allocation:** Setting aside a fixed amount each month.

- **Percentage of Revenue:** Allocating a specific percentage of your monthly revenue for repairs.
- **Emergency Fund:** Creating an emergency fund specifically for repairs that can be tapped into when needed.

It's advisable to combine these methods. For example, you could set aside a fixed monthly amount and allocate a small percentage of your revenue to your emergency repair fund. You'll get a much better understanding of these costs as you go along, so start by at least considering a percentage of your revenue to repairs and maintenance. We'll further explore budgeting in Chapter 10 as part of our discussion on financial management.

CHAPTER 7

SUPPLIERS

You'll be interacting with suppliers practically daily. The types of products you source and from whom can significantly impact the success of your business. Failure to manage this relationship correctly could result in empty machines, unhappy customers, and declining profits. Let's get to know them better.

7.1 Types of Suppliers

Wholesalers:

- **Key Features:** They offer a wide variety of products at a discounted rate, making them ideal for vending machine businesses that provide multiple types of products.
- **Advantages:** Buying in bulk at discounted prices can improve profit margins and provide your customers diverse offerings.

Manufacturers:

- **Key Features:** If you're looking to specialize in a particular type of product, it might be more cost-effective to buy directly from the manufacturer.
- **Advantages:** Cutting out the middleman can reduce costs and ensure a direct supply of specific products tailored to your vending business.

Don't be afraid to buy products at your supermarket and test them out. It's the quickest way to understand your consumer's preference and then move on to finding the ideal supplier.

7.2 How to Find a Supplier

Thorough research saves you from future headaches. Read reviews, ask for references, and visit the operation centers of the suppliers you consider. Trade shows and online directories can also be gold mines of information.

Qualities to Look for in a Supplier

- **Reliability**: Your supplier must be able to deliver products on time, every time.
- **Communication**: Ensure they are interested in generating a healthy commercial relationship with your company.
- **Quality & Pricing**: Sub-par products will damage your reputation and drive customers away. The more affordable, the better—don't compromise on quality.
- **Flexibility**: Business can be unpredictable. Your supplier should be able to adapt to your changing needs.

Sample before your source

Once you've shortlisted potential suppliers, the next step is sampling. Never skip this phase. Knowing firsthand the quality you're bringing to your customers is essential. Request samples and test them for taste, quality, and shelf life.

Always Have a Backup

It's wise to have a backup supplier for critical items. Whether due to shipping delays, quality issues, or other unforeseen challenges, relying on a single supplier can sometimes backfire.

7.3: Negotiating with Suppliers

So, you've found potential suppliers and sampled their products: the next phase—negotiation. Negotiating with suppliers isn't just about pushing for the lowest price. It's about striking a deal that benefits both parties, securing a quality product, and establishing terms that make your vending machine business sustainable and profitable.

Consider terms like minimum order quantities, payment terms, and delivery schedules. Remember, a good deal is a balanced deal. While cost is undoubtedly a factor, the reliability of a supplier is equally important. Vending is such a day-to-day operation a dependable supplier with competitive prices surpasses an inconsistent supplier with cheap products.

Know Your Numbers

Before entering negotiations, you must be armed with data. Know your target sales price, desired profit margin, and the maximum cost per unit you can afford. Without these numbers, you'll be negotiating in the dark.

Price Negotiation

While everyone wants the lowest price, an unfairly low price can compromise quality or reliability. Instead of merely asking for a discount, discuss how you can work together to lower costs. This could be through bulk purchasing, long-term contracts, credit, or waiving specific additional fees. Most suppliers often tailor their prices based on the agreed-upon conditions and the client-supplier relationship.

You also need to consider various costs beyond the product's unit price. These can include shipping fees, taxes, and storage.

Terms and Conditions

The agreed terms and conditions matter just as much as the price. Take into account the following:

- **Payment Terms**: Agree on a payment schedule that works for your cash flow. Net-30 or Net-60 terms are standard.
- **Minimum Order Quantity (MOQ)**: If the supplier's MOQ is too high for your initial needs, try negotiating for a smaller initial order with the agreement to scale up later.
- **Lead Times**: Confirm that the provider can satisfy your delivery requirements (weekly, monthly?).
- **Returns**: It's a tough one, but if possible, aim to incorporate terms allowing returns for testing and potential product exchanges based on performance in your vending machine.

Building a Relationship

Long-term success in the vending machine business isn't just about transactions; it's about building relationships. Building a robust and long-term relationship with your supplier can offer significant benefits, such as more favorable terms, priority service, and insights into new products or market trends. Keep lines of communication open, pay your bills on time, and always be professional.

Legal Considerations

While verbal agreements can be enforceable, getting all negotiated terms in writing is crucial. A formal contract is a reference and a legal safeguard for both parties. Consider involving a legal advisor experienced in contract law to review the terms.

Ensure you understand the legal aspects of sourcing. Read the fine print on contracts, understand return policies, and ensure no hidden clauses could be detrimental to you.

7.4: Supplier Assessment Worksheet— Pricing and Payment Terms Template

By this point in your journey, you've scouted potential suppliers and even entered preliminary negotiations. But how do you compare them effectively? That's where a Supplier Assessment Worksheet, focusing on pricing and payment terms, comes into play. Not only will this tool help you keep track of the details involved, but it will also help you to make an informed decision. Let's explore how to create and utilize this worksheet.

What Goes into the Worksheet?

Your worksheet should offer a clear, side-by-side comparison of potential suppliers, focusing on crucial aspects that impact your bottom line. Here are the core elements:

- **Supplier Name**: Clearly state the supplier's name for easy identification.
- **Product Price**: Note the per-unit price of the products you intend to source.
- **Minimum Order Quantity (MOQ)**: Indicate the minimum number of products you must purchase per order.
- **Payment Terms**: Include each supplier's payment terms (Net-30, Net-60, etc.).

- **Discount Structure**: Outline any volume-based or long-term contractual discounts.
- **Additional Costs**: Note any extra costs like shipping, handling, or taxes.
- **Total Landed Cost**: Calculate the total cost to get the product to your warehouse or directly to the vending machine.
- **Lead Time**: The time the supplier takes to deliver after placing an order.
- **Payment Methods**: Types of payments accepted (e.g., credit card, wire transfer, etc.).

How to Use the Worksheet

Fill in the information for each supplier as you conduct your research and negotiations. Use the worksheet as a dynamic tool; update it whenever you get new information. Here's how to make the most out of your worksheet:

- **Rate Suppliers**: After filling in all the information, you could also rate suppliers based on your priorities. For example, if the payment terms are crucial for your cash flow, give higher weight to suppliers offering favorable terms.
- **Spot Red Flags**: Glaring inconsistencies between suppliers in areas like pricing could be a warning sign that requires further investigation.
- **Identify Bargaining Points**: Knowing multiple suppliers' average prices and terms can give you a stronger negotiating position.

- **Shortlist Candidates**: Use the worksheet to narrow your list to the most promising suppliers for the next round of in-depth evaluations or negotiations.

Worksheet Template

While the exact requirements can vary from business to business, a simple template might look something like this:

Supplier Name	Product Price	MOQ	Payment Terms	Discounts	Additional Costs	Total Landed Cost	Lead Time	Payment Methods
Supplier A								

Once a supplier is chosen, a comparable worksheet can be employed to track and manage agreed conditions, prices, and other relevant information, allowing you to generate an accurate monthly financial projection.

CHAPTER 8

STOCKING & INVENTORY MANAGEMENT

Inventory management isn't just about filling your machines with snacks, beverages, or other items. It's a delicate balancing act of offering the right product mix, forecasting demand, managing stock levels, and ensuring optimal turnover rates. Poor inventory management can lead to expired products, out-of-stock situations, and ultimately, unsatisfied customers and lost revenue.

8.1: Managing Inventory Efficiently

Being efficient in your inventory management can save you time, money, and a whole lot of headaches. Efficiency here means minimizing waste—in the form of expired products, overstocking, or frequent stockouts. When you are efficient, your vending machines turn over inventory faster, which means more revenue and less spoilage.

Methods of Inventory Tracking

How you track and control your stock matters significantly. Here are three essential methods:

- **Manual Count:** The most straightforward but most time-consuming method. Requires physical counts of the stock in each machine.

- **Barcode Scanning:** A step up in terms of efficiency. Use a barcode scanner to manage inventory levels.
- **Smart Vending Machines:** These machines offer real-time tracking and can even send you alerts when stock levels are low.

Implementing the ABC Analysis

The ABC analysis is a business model used to classify inventory into three categories based on their importance:

- **A-items:** High-value products that require regular monitoring.
- **B-items:** Medium-value products that need less frequent attention.
- **C-items:** Low-value products that require minimal oversight.

By categorizing your items, you can allocate your resources more efficiently. For instance, you may check the stock levels of A-items every day, B-items every week, and C-items every month.

It's crucial to prioritize A-items as they are fast-selling and contribute significantly to your revenue stream while minimizing the risk of spoilage or expiry. However, don't overlook C-items items entirely— sometimes, they serve as an essential part of your product mix and cater to niche customer needs.

As a helpful reference, your top 1 or 2 A-items should account for at least 20% of your total sales, emphasizing the need to keep them well-stocked and monitored. This strategic categorization ensures a streamlined and cost-effective approach to inventory management.

Forecasting Demand

Forecasting demand is a vital aspect of inventory management. Analyzing sales trends empowers you to make informed decisions on stocking levels. Here's how you can enhance this process:

Detailed Sales Data

Keep a comprehensive record of sales data for each machine, including product-wise sales and timestamps. This data will serve as the foundation for insightful analysis.

Pattern Recognition

Dive into the data to identify patterns and trends. For instance, observe if sales of hot beverages surge during colder months or if a specific snack is popular during exam periods at nearby college campuses.

Seasonal Adjustments

Tailor your inventory based on seasonal variations. Adjust stock levels accordingly for products that observe seasonal demand shifts. Cold beverages might be in higher demand during summer, while warm snacks might see increased sales in winter. Are there certain products that perform better during the holidays?

Promotions and Events

Monitor how promotions or events in the vicinity impact sales. If a local event attracts a larger audience, adjust your stock accordingly to meet the potential surge in demand.

Customer Preferences

Leverage insights into customer preferences. Analyze which products are consistently popular and which ones are losing traction. Adjust your stocking strategy to align with these preferences.

By leveraging this sales analysis, you can anticipate demand patterns, ensuring your inventory is efficiently stocked to meet customer needs while minimizing unnecessary costs.

Automate Wherever Possible

Consider investing in inventory management software that can connect to your vending machines. These systems can notify you when it's time to reorder supplies or when a specific item isn't selling as well as expected. Automation reduces human error and frees up time for you to focus on other areas of your business.

Reducing Shrinkage

Shrinkage refers to inventory loss due to theft, damage, or wastage. While you can't eliminate shrinkage entirely, you can reduce it with proactive measures. Conduct regular and thorough audits of your machines to identify any discrepancies promptly. Implement tamper-proof mechanisms to deter theft and vandalism. Cultivate strong relationships with location owners, fostering a sense of mutual responsibility for machine security. A comprehensive approach encompassing audits, security measures, and stakeholder collaboration is crucial in effectively managing inventory shrinkage.

8.2: Avoiding Overstock and Understock

Inventory mismanagement can come in two forms: overstock and understock. Both can derail your profit margins and affect your business in ways you may have yet to consider. Let's explore these issues in detail and discuss strategies to avoid them.

What Is Overstocking and Why Is It Bad?

Overstocking happens when you have too much product in your storage or vending machines. You might think, "The more the merrier!" But this approach has several downsides:

- **Expiry Dates:** Many vending machine items have a limited shelf life. Overstocking increases the likelihood of products expiring before they can be sold.
- **Storage Costs:** If you're storing excess stock in a warehouse or even your garage, you're incurring additional expenses that cut into your profits.
- **Cash Flow:** Overstocking means tying up money in products that aren't selling fast enough. This affects your cash flow, limiting your ability to invest in other areas of your business.

- **Market Trends:** Consumer preferences change. You'll face losses if you're overstocked on an item that suddenly falls out of favor.

What Is Understocking and Why Is It Also Bad?

Understocking is the opposite issue. It occurs when you need more products to meet demand. While it may sound like a better problem to have, understocking also has its downsides:

- **Lost Sales:** An empty slot in your vending machine is a lost sales opportunity.
- **Customer Dissatisfaction:** Consistently understocked machines can frustrate customers, leading them to seek alternatives.
- **Operational Costs:** If you're constantly restocking, you're spending more time and money on operations than you should be.

Strategies to Avoid Overstock and Understock

Now that we know why overstocking and understocking are bad, how can we avoid them? Here are some actionable strategies:

Data-Driven Decision Making

For those using smart vending machines, take advantage of the built-in sophisticated software that tracks sales data, allowing you to gain insights into consumer preferences and make informed decisions on restocking. However, implementing a manual tracking system is key if you're operating without a smart vending machine. Keep a record of daily sales for each product to understand what's selling well. While not as automated, this data will provide valuable insights into popular items and guide your restocking decisions, ensuring you tailor your approach to your vending business's specific technology capabilities.

Optimize Reorder Points

The moment at which you reorder stock is crucial for keeping your vending machines running smoothly. A practical approach is calculating the lead time demand—how many items you'll need during the time it takes for a new order to arrive. This number helps you set the reorder point effectively. A general guideline is reordering a product when its stock level reaches 30-50% of its initial inventory. However, this percentage may vary depending on the product's popularity and shelf life.

First-In, First-Out

The 'First-In, First-Out' (FIFO) strategy is often the best practice for stock rotation. Regularly check product expiry dates and ensure items with the earliest expiry dates are positioned at the front of the machine. The last thing you want is for a consumer to receive an out-of-date product. This method minimizes waste and reduces the risk of overstocking perishables, contributing to efficient inventory management and maintaining customer satisfaction by delivering fresh products. Continuously rotate your stock so that items with the earliest expiry dates are sold first.

Seasonal Adjustments

Some items sell better during certain seasons. Keep this in mind when stocking. For example, cold beverages might sell more in the summer, while hot chocolate could be a hit in the winter.

Just-In-Time (JIT) Inventory

Adopting a JIT approach can help minimize storage costs and reduce the chances of overstocking. This means you only order and store products that you'll sell in the near term. Doing so minimizes storage costs and the risk of overstocking items that might sell slowly.

In a JIT system, you order products just in time to meet demand, reducing the need for excess inventory. However, it's prudent to maintain a "safety stock," a small reserve inventory to cover unexpected spikes in demand or delays in restocking. This safety net ensures you can meet customer needs even during unforeseen circumstances, balancing efficient inventory management and customer satisfaction.

CHAPTER 9

MANAGING OPERATIONS

In this chapter, we'll explore the key operational aspects you should focus on to ensure long-term success. Before we get into specifics, let's begin by highlighting three foundational pillars every operation should include:

1. Daily Monitoring

Daily monitoring is critical. Track stock levels, machine performance, and sales data in real time. This enables swift responses to issues such as out-of-stock products or machine malfunctions, minimizing downtimes and revenue loss, and allows you to make informed and strategic operational decisions. We'll discuss the KPIs (Key Performance Indicators) you should track later in this chapter.

2. Periodic Servicing

Regular servicing is more than just restocking. It includes cleaning the machines, checking for wear and tear, ensuring the coin and note acceptors are working correctly, and other maintenance tasks. Create a maintenance and cleaning schedule and stick to it religiously.

3. Record-Keeping

Accurate and meticulous record-keeping is vital for any business.

Maintain logs of everything from restocking and cash collection to machine servicing and repair. Proper records not only help in effective management but are also crucial for tax purposes.

9.1: Daily Operations Checklist

When discussing managing operations, you may wonder: Where do I start each day? What should I look at first? A daily operations checklist will help you map each day correctly and ensure nothing slips through the cracks.

A daily operations checklist is more than just a to-do list; it's your strategic tool to streamline operations, enhance efficiency, and increase your bottom line. As your vending business grows, this checklist should become invaluable to your daily routine.

Vital details can often and inadvertently be overlooked. A checklist is a fail-safe system to ensure you accomplish everything necessary for your business's smooth functioning daily.

The Checklist

1. **Inventory Check:** Use your inventory management software or spreadsheet to review stock levels in each machine. Make a list of items that need to be restocked.
2. **Sales Review:** Analyze the previous day's sales to identify trends or standout products. Are some items selling better at certain times or locations?
3. **Cash Collection:** Plan for the cash to be collected from the

machines. Depending on the foot traffic, some machines might need more frequent collection.

4. **Machine Inspections:** Review the status of your machines, replenish, check the cleaning schedule, and see if any malfunctioning units need immediate attention (execute your Preventive Maintenance Checklist as we discussed in Chapter 6)

5. **Customer Feedback:** Check emails, social media, or other channels for customer feedback and reviews. Talk with the location manager to ensure no issues have been reported. Take any required corrective measures.

6. **Supplier Contact:** If your stock levels are running low, contact your suppliers to place orders.

7. **Employee/Contractor Communication:** If you have staff or contractors, communicate special instructions or updates.

Automating the Checklist

While a physical checklist is good, an automated system is even better. Use tools like task management software or specialized vending machine operation software to keep track of your daily operations. These tools often have features like reminders and alerts to ensure you don't miss critical tasks.

Customizing Your Checklist

Every vending machine business is unique, and you may need to add or remove items from your daily checklist accordingly. For example, if you also offer perishable items, you may need to include a daily check for expired products.

9.2 Cash Handling

Although digital payments are gaining more and more ground, cash remains a significant part of vending machine transactions, and it's an essential operational issue. Develop a secure and efficient cash collection, counting, and depositing system. Ensure that only authorized personnel handle cash and maintain stringent accountability standards.

Efficient Collection Strategies

Designate optimal collection times and routes based on machine traffic. Utilize smart, safe tech for secure in-machine cash validation and storage, reducing exposure. If you don't need to count coins, you could deposit directly to the bank once you finish your route.

Secure Storage

Implement secure storage within machines, like drop safes, accessible only to authorized personnel. Use robust locking mechanisms to deter theft.

Regular Cash Counting and Reconciliation

Schedule routine cash counts, reconciling with sales records to promptly identify discrepancies. Involve at least two employees for accuracy and transparency.

Access Controls and Authorization

Enforce a strict access policy for cash handling. Authorized, trained employees should exclusively handle cash. Use unique access codes/keys for tracking and monitoring.

9.3: Dealing with Common Issues

Even with your daily checklist and the best planning, problems will inevitably happen. Let's review some of the most common issues vending machine operators face and how to address them effectively.

Machine Malfunctions

Machine breakdowns are uncomfortable and bound to harm your reputation and cost you repeat business. Regular preventive maintenance is essential. Also, having a reliable repair service on speed dial can save you in emergencies. Always communicate by posting a notice on the machine informing customers about the malfunction and the expected repair time.

Stockouts

Having an empty slot in your vending machine is just bad business. Stockouts can occur for various reasons, including poor inventory management or unexpected demand for a particular item.

Use your spreadsheet or technology to monitor stock levels in real time, set up alerts where possible, and regularly review your sales data to predict future stockouts.

Theft and Vandalism

There is no escaping vandalism and theft in vending. Whether it's someone trying to break into the machine or simply damaging it, these acts will more than likely have a financial impact.

The best solution is prevention. Pick your location with this in mind; pick an area with good natural surveillance from passersby or security staff, which also tends to have lower incidences of theft and vandalism.

If problems persist, request a new location from your provider. If you are having issues with theft or vandalism and don't want to move your machine, you could also invest in security cameras – even fake ones and place anti-theft stickers on your machines as a deterrent.

Outdated Products

Products close to or past their expiration date can be a health risk and a liability. Regular inspections are a must. Use First-In-First-Out (FIFO) methods to ensure that older stock is sold before newer items. When restocking, always check the expiry dates.

Payment Issues

From coin jams to failed card transactions, this will probably be your most common issue, and payment issues can frustrate customers and lead to lost sales and recurring customers.

Test the payment mechanisms regularly during routine maintenance visits and monitor customer complaints. Modern vending machines have remote monitoring features that alert you about payment issues in real-time.

Negative Customer Feedback

No business is immune to negative feedback. In the vending machine industry, from issues with change to product quality problems, complaints can vary. Address complaints promptly and professionally.

Use the feedback to improve your services, and consider offering refunds or free products as a goodwill gesture. Find more insights on this topic in Chapter 12.

9.4 Key Performance Indicators (KPIs) for Operations

When it comes to effectively managing vending machine operations, monitoring and analyzing key performance indicators (KPIs) is crucial. These KPIs provide valuable insights into your operations, helping you make informed decisions and optimize your product management. Here are some essential KPIs to keep in mind:

Sales Volume:

What is it? The total sales within a specific time period.

Formula: `Total sales revenue during that time`

How to Measure: Calculate the total revenue generated from sales within the chosen time frame.

Average Transaction Value (ATV):

What is it? The average value of each transaction.

Formula: `Total sales revenue / Number of transactions`

How to Measure: Divide the total revenue generated by the number of transactions to get the average transaction value.

Machine Uptime Rate:

What is it? The percentage of time machines are operational.

Formula: `(Total time machines are operational / Total time) × 100`

How to Measure: Measure the total time your vending machines were operational and divide it by the total time, then multiply by 100 to get the percentage.

Stockout Rate:

What is it? The rate at which stockouts occur.

Formula: `(Number of times stockouts occur) / (Total number of transactions) × 100`

How to Measure: Count the number of times stockouts occur and divide it by the total number of transactions. Multiply by 100 to get the percentage.

Product Popularity Index:

What is it? The popularity of a specific product based on its sales.

Formula: `(Number of times a product is sold) / (Total products sold) × 100`

How to Measure: Count the number of times a specific product is sold and divide it by the total products sold. Multiply by 100 to get the percentage representing the product's popularity.

CHAPTER 10

FINANCIAL MANAGEMENT

Cash flow is king. No matter how amazing your vending machine locations are or how great your product mix is, you're in for a world of hurt if you can't manage your finances. This chapter will review the financial aspects you should always pay attention to.

Managing finances may not be the most exciting part of running a vending machine business, but it's undeniably one of the most important. Efficient financial management enables you to make informed decisions, plan for the future, and, more importantly, ensure that your business remains profitable.

Financial Planning

A financial plan provides a roadmap for your business, showing you where you are, where you want to go, and how you intend to get there. When creating a financial plan:

- Define your revenue streams and set your pricing strategy.
- Identify fixed and variable expenses to estimate your break-even point.
- Plan for contingencies, like unexpected repairs or seasonal fluctuations.

Working Capital

Working capital is the lifeline of any business and refers to the money you use in the day-to-day operations. With vending machines, this includes cash for restocking inventory, machine repairs, lease payments, and ensuring you have change available for customers in each machine.

When considering working capital for your vending machine business, it's crucial to factor in the funds necessary for providing change to customers. A significant portion of vending machine transactions will probably be using cash, and ensuring that your machines always has change is essential for customer satisfaction and repeat business.

Ensure you always maintain a sufficient working capital reserve to cover these ongoing expenses and any unexpected costs that may arise during your operations. A well-managed working capital ensures that your vending machine business remains operational and can seize growth opportunities.

Financial Statements

You don't need to be an accountant to understand the basics of financial statements. Familiarize yourself with:

- **Income Statement:** Shows your revenues, expenses, and profits or losses over a period.
- **Balance Sheet:** A snapshot of your assets, liabilities, and equity at a specific time.

- **Cash Flow Statement:** Highlights how changes in the balance sheet and income statements affect cash.

Tax Management

Managing your taxes efficiently can save you a lot of money. Consult with a tax advisor to understand the deductions you can claim, and always set aside a percentage of your income for tax purposes. This will help you avoid unpleasant surprises during tax season.

Properly tracking income and expenses has tax benefits. You can accurately calculate your tax liabilities and even discover deductions you may have missed. Consult a tax advisor for guidance specific to your situation.

10.1: Tracking Income and Expenses

The real game-changer is how well you manage your income and expenses. This will guide you through the best practices for tracking your financials effectively. Without accurate tracking, you're operating in the dark.

The Basics of Income Tracking

Income from a vending machine business is straightforward: the money you make from selling products. However, you need to keep track of:

- **Daily Sales:** The amount you make each day from each

machine.

- **Product-Specific Income:** How much you earn from different types of products. This helps in future inventory decisions.
- **Additional Income:** Money earned from secondary sources like advertising on your machine.

Calculating Daily Sales

Daily Sales are calculated by multiplying the number of units of each product sold by their respective prices.

```
Daily sales = Units of each product sold × product price
```

It would be best to distinguish the cash you collect from daily sales. Collected cash includes the additional money when giving change, while the remaining cash in your machine is for providing change. This requires diligent tracking, especially if you accept cash and card payments. You must maintain close control over the money flowing into your business.

Expense Tracking 101

Expenses are trickier to manage. They can broadly be categorized into:

- **Fixed Costs:** These are inescapable costs like machine leases, rent for the space, and utility bills.
- **Variable Costs:** These include the cost of inventory, fuel for transportation, and maintenance.
- **Unexpected Costs:** Breakdowns, vandalism, and other

unforeseen expenses.

General Expenses Per Machine

Consider these general expenses per machine as a foundational guide, which may vary based on machine specifics:

One-time Costs

- **Initial Investment:** This could be a one-time payment for a machine or a monthly leasing fee.
- **Machine Setup:** The cost of setting up your vending machine, configuring the trays and spirals for your product mix, and any branding you want to use.
- **Installation/Removal:** This is the transportation costs from your warehouse to the location. This would depend on the area and logistics involved.

Cost Per Machine

- **Location Fee:** If applicable, limit this to 10% of total sales as a prudent approach to ensure profitability.
- **Preventive & Corrective Maintenance:** Fixed fee divided by the total number of machines.
- **Replenishment:** You should consider an average of 10-15% of total sales, contingent on location and visitation frequency.

Financial Aspects

- **Card Payment Fees:** Usually range from 1% to 3% of total sales.

- **Surprise and Vandalism Fund:** Allocating 10% of total sales for unexpected events is a reasonable contingency fund to cover unforeseen costs like vandalism or urgent repairs.
- **Product Margin:** Maintaining a 40% margin for product costs is a decent target to ensure profitability and cover other expenses.
- **Administrative and Sales Costs:** Covering administrative, accounting, and non-operational staff expenses.

10.2 Financial Ratios

Financial ratios help in analyzing profitability, efficiency, and overall financial health. Here are some essential financial ratios and how to calculate and interpret them:

Return on Investment (ROI):

What is it? ROI measures the return generated on the investment made in your vending machine business. It indicates how efficiently you're utilizing your investment to generate profits.

Formula: `(Net Profit / Total Investment) × 100`

How to Measure: Calculate your net profit (total revenue minus total expenses) and divide it by the total investment (initial setup costs, operational costs, etc.). Multiply by 100 to get the percentage.

Profit Margin:

What is it? Profit margin assesses the percentage of total revenue that translates into profit. It reflects the efficiency of your business in controlling costs and generating earnings.

Formula: `(Net Profit / Total Revenue) × 100`

How to Measure: Calculate your net profit (total revenue minus total expenses) and divide it by the total revenue. Multiply by 100 to get the percentage.

Gross Margin:

What is it? Gross margin measures the profitability of individual products by considering the difference between the cost of goods sold and the revenue generated from sales.

Formula: `((Total Revenue - Cost of Goods Sold) / Total Revenue) × 100`

How to Measure: Subtract the cost of goods sold from total revenue, divide this by total revenue, and then multiply by 100 to get the percentage.

Liquidity Ratios (e.g., Current Ratio):

What is it? Liquidity ratios evaluate the ability of your business to meet short-term financial obligations. The current ratio explicitly assesses your business's capacity to cover short-term debts with its current assets.

Formula: `Current Assets / Current Liabilities`

How to Measure: Divide the total current assets (cash, accounts receivable, etc.) by the total current liabilities (short-term debts, payables, etc.).

Debt-to-Equity Ratio:

What is it? The debt-to-equity ratio illustrates the proportion of your business's financing from debt instead of equity. It helps in evaluating the financial leverage and risk exposure of your business.

Formula: `Total Debt / Total Equity`

How to Measure: Divide the business's total debt by the total equity.

Inventory Turnover Ratio:

What is it? This ratio gauges how quickly your inventory is being sold and replaced. A high turnover ratio indicates efficient inventory management.

Formula: `Cost of Goods Sold / Average Inventory`

How to Measure: Calculate the cost of goods sold and divide it by the average inventory value (beginning inventory + ending inventory / 2).

10.3: Maximizing Profitability

While tracking income and expenses sets the stage, the real showstopper in your vending machine business is how you maximize profitability. You know how to calculate your profit margin and how much is coming in. You have two options to maximize profit: sell more or spend less.

Selling more

You can improve your income stream with different strategies like dynamic pricing or a secondary income stream like branding your machine with advertising.

Spending less

Financial management generally requires you to find ways to reduce your operational costs as it directly impacts profitability. Efficiency is profitability's best friend. The less time and resources you spend operating your business, the higher your potential profit. This could mean optimizing your route, automating systems, or negotiating with suppliers or locations for lower prices. But beware an excessive focus on cost-cutting may compromise the quality of the product and service you offer. There is no easier way to lose customers than to show a dip in service — Striking the right balance is crucial.

10.2: Keeping a Budget for Surprises

If there's one universal truth in business, it's that surprises are inevitable. When operating a vending machine business, these surprises can range from minor hiccups like machine malfunctions to more severe incidents like theft or vandalism. While you can't eliminate surprises, you can definitely prepare for them. And that starts with budgeting. Let's explore why keeping a budget for surprises is essential and how to do it effectively.

How much should I budget for surprises?

A general rule of thumb is to set aside at least 10-20% of your monthly operational costs as a 'surprises budget.' The actual cost, however, will vary depending on the size and scale of your organization.

Types of Surprises to Budget For

- **Machine Repairs:** No matter how diligent you are with maintenance, machines can still break down unexpectedly. These repairs can often be costly.
- **Stock Wastage:** Issues like expired products or potential stock theft can be costly surprises.
- **Legal Fees:** Whether it's permit issues or a liability lawsuit, legal troubles can come out of nowhere and often come with steep fees.
- **Emergency Relocation:** Sometimes, you may have to move a machine with little notice due to construction or changes in

location policies.

Can insurance cover some of these surprises?

Yes, certain types of insurance, like liability and property, can cover some surprises, such as repair due to vandalism. However, not everything is insurable; even when it is, claiming insurance can be time-consuming. Carefully assess your insurance coverage and understand its terms and limitations to protect you against potential surprises.

How to Create a 'Surprises Budget'

So, how do you go about creating a budget for surprises? The steps are similar to creating any other type of budget but with a few unique considerations.

- **Analyze Past Incidents:** Go through your records and identify any unexpected costs you've incurred in the past. This can give you a good idea of what surprises to anticipate.
- **Estimate Costs:** Once you know what to expect, estimate how much each type of surprise could potentially cost you.
- **Set Aside Funds:** Set aside a dedicated fund based on your estimates. Make this a separate account to avoid the temptation of using these funds for regular operations.
- **Review and Adjust:** Review this budget. Your potential for surprises (and their costs) may change as your business grows and evolves.

CHAPTER 11

MARKETING & ATTRACTING CUSTOMERS

Contrary to popular belief, vending machines don't always sell themselves. Just because your machine is out there doesn't mean people will automatically start buying. Effective marketing can help you create awareness, build trust, and encourage repeat business.

11.1 Methods of Attracting Customers

As mentioned earlier in Chapter 4, one of your first steps is to figure out who you're marketing to. Are your main clients students, office professionals, or travelers? Understanding your target demographic will help drive your marketing plan; here are a few ways to attract that audience.

Strategic Placement

Visibility is vital – if they can't see you, you don't exist. Your vending machine's location serves as a fundamental marketing tool. Place your machines where they are easily visible and accessible to your target audience. Make sure your machine is clean, attractive, and *pops* as much as possible. Over time, you may also want to explore the effect on sales by moving your vending machine to a different location within a building.

Promotions and Discounts

While not particularly glamorous, mastering vending machine marketing boils down to a fundamental principle: be either ultra-convenient (with no comparable alternatives nearby) or capture your audience's attention through price. So, if you have a lot of competition around that, you have a few products where your profit margin might narrow, but in return, the attraction for customers will be high. You can also offer limited-time promotions and discounts to entice people to try your products or offer sudden, short-term flash deals clearly announced with branding on the machine itself. People love a good deal; the urgency will drive them to your vending machine. Also, align your product offerings with seasons. You could offer holiday-themed snacks during Christmas or cold beverages at discounted prices during summer.

Branding and Partnerships

As we said above, make your machine stand out as much as possible. Your vending machine should reflect your brand's colors, logo, and other elements that make it unique. Strong branding can bring you awareness. To help finance this kind of branding, you could collaborate with suppliers for co-branding opportunities, sharing expenses, and creating a visually appealing machine that entices customers; imagine a Kit-Kat branded machine, for example.

Social Media and Online Presence

Despite what most will probably say, social media isn't always the answer. It's going to depend on the uniqueness of your machine and products. If you are a traditional snack or beverage machine, all your energy should be focused on attracting customers with reasonable prices and a well-polished machine. But if you have a smart vending machine or a unique product, social media may help you get the word out. Utilize platforms like Instagram, Twitter, and Facebook to create an online presence. You can post regular updates, promotions, and even customer testimonials to attract a broader audience.

Leveraging Smart Vending Technology for Enhanced Engagement

For advanced smart vending businesses, integrating a mobile payment system into your machines offers customers convenient payment options and the opportunity to utilize transaction data for a personalized experience.

Perks Tailored for Office Environments

Smart vending technology, especially pertinent in office settings, allows for the integration of exclusive perks. Companies employing this vending service can offer their employees a monthly quota, making the vending experience convenient and a workplace benefit. The seamless mobile payment system facilitates effortless transactions, enhancing employee satisfaction within the office ecosystem.

This service could pave the way for loyalty programs. Integrated within a mobile app, this program can reward customers with points or exclusive deals for each transaction, encouraging continued engagement.

Make the most of the payment app

The mobile app also serves as a central hub, displaying vending machine locations, available products, and ongoing promotions, keeping customers informed and enticed to choose your vending machines over alternatives. Push notifications through the app can further alert customers about new offers, creating a sense of excitement and encouraging repeat business.

11.2 Measuring Marketing Effectiveness

In Chapter 9, we explored operational KPIs. Now, let's complement that with KPIs tailored for assessing marketing strategies. Here are some practical KPIs along with easy-to-understand explanations, formulas for calculation, and applicability based on payment systems:

Customer Retention Rate:

What is it? The percentage of customers you keep over a period.

Formula: `((Customers at the end - Customers acquired) / Customers at the start)) × 100`.

How to Measure: Count the number of customers at the start and end of a specific time period. Subtract the customers acquired during that time from the total at the end, then divide this by the customers at the start. Multiply by 100 to get the percentage.

A/B Testing:

How to use? Test different product placements, prices, or promotions to see what works best.

How to Measure: Conduct controlled experiments by presenting different versions (A and B) of a product, price, or promotion to two comparable groups of customers. Measure the response and analyze which version performs better.

Customer Satisfaction Score (CSAT):

What is it? A way to know how happy your customers are.

Formula: `(Sum of all customer satisfaction ratings) / (Number of customers).`

How to measure? Conduct customer surveys to gather feedback and insights for refining marketing strategies and product offerings when possible. Survey them after their purchase and give the customer a free product in gratitude. If you have emails or offer a machine in an office or gym, see if the location provider can help you reach your audience to improve your service.

Customer Acquisition Cost (CAC) and Customer Lifetime Value (CLV)

Fundamental indicators that are possible to calculate with individual customer identification. So, typically, it is only possible for transactions with cards or mobile apps.

CAC - What did it cost to get a customer?

Formula: `Total costs for getting customers / Number of new custcmers (or transaction count within a specific time).`

CLV - How valuable is a customer to your business?

Formula: Average purchase value × Number of repeat purchases × Average time a customer stays.

CHAPTER 12

CUSTOMER SERVICE

In the vending business, customer service bridges the customer and your machines—every interaction, from the initial engagement to handling complaints. The vending machine itself might be the 'face' of your business, but customer service is the personality that defines how customers perceive your brand.

A well-structured customer service approach ensures customers have a seamless experience with your machines. It involves giving clear purchase instructions, timely restocking of products, machine maintenance, addressing concerns, and providing a pleasant overall experience. Customers should feel valued and attended to, even in a seemingly self-service environment. A satisfied customer is more likely to become a loyal one and recommend your vending service to others.

12.1: Making the customer feel safe

Everyone who has ever used a vending machine has their share of negative experiences, who hasn't got their money stuck or their candy failing to dispense. No matter how sophisticated your machine is, it will have issues, and there will be no one near for the customer to complain to. It's vital to make customers feel safe and secure in their interactions with your machines and, above all, to make them feel like they will get a quick solution to the problem they just had.

In response to these concerns, some businesses have swiftly

introduced "guaranteed cash returns" to address such issues. This offers a sense of security to customers, assuring them that, in case of any problem, customers can call a dedicated number, and the business will quickly address the issue, including refunding the affected amount. However, implementing such a system requires robust fraud prevention measures to maintain the system's integrity and prevent misuse (no one taking advantage of some free cash).

While offering this level of security is a valuable customer service initiative, evaluating its financial feasibility is equally essential. Assessing if your cash flow allows for such guarantees and balancing the cost against the benefit of providing this security is a strategic decision. Allocating the budget for this refund measure from the marketing budget can be a viable approach, ensuring a balance between customer satisfaction and operational costs.

12.2: A customer-centric approach

Creating a genuine connection between customers and vending machines poses a significant challenge for customer service in the vending industry. The key to overcoming this challenge lies in adopting a customer-centric strategy, where every aspect of your vending business is centered around how you make your customers feel.

To instill a customer-first mindset within your vending business, prioritize customer satisfaction at every level. It starts by ensuring your team possesses comprehensive product knowledge, practical communication skills, and conflict-resolution abilities. A broad understanding of every business element provides they can assist customers effectively.

The ultimate goal is to craft an environment where the customer feels heard, valued, safe, and prioritized throughout their vending experience. By enhancing the overall vending experience, you can bridge the gap between the seemingly automated nature of vending machines and the personalized touch that customers appreciate. You can transform a mere transaction into a positive and memorable interaction through a customer-centric approach.

12.3: Effective Communication with Customers

Regarding instructions and general communication on your machine, it's essential to acknowledge that customers often skim or overlook instructions or, better said, they do not read. Customers appreciate clear and straightforward communication. Ensure that instructions on using the vending machine and contact information for support are visible and as concise as possible. If any issues arise, transparently communicate the steps being taken to resolve them and provide a timeline for resolution.

In the event of any issues, transparency is crucial. Communicate openly about the steps being taken to resolve problems and provide a clear timeline for resolution. Prompt responses to customer inquiries or complaints are equally vital. Acknowledge their concerns immediately and keep them informed throughout the resolution process. A delayed response can lead to frustration and a negative perception of your business. On the contrary, a well-maintained communication channel can surprisingly be an effective marketing tool, fostering trust and loyalty among your customer base.

12.4: Leveraging Technology for Enhanced Customer Service

If your vending machine has digital platforms like a payment app or smart vending interaction, you can harness user data and preferences. This allows you to personalize offers, making customers feel a sense of familiarity with the machine—a vital aspect of positive customer interaction.

Suppose you have a loyalty program integrated into these platforms. In that case, it not only provides a communication channel with customers but also enables you to offer refunds and tailored incentives, encouraging repeat purchases and reinforcing customer satisfaction.

These tech-driven strategies can significantly elevate your vending business's customer service standards.

CHAPTER 13

SCALING YOUR VENDING BUSINESS

Once you've optimized your operations and are enjoying a steady income, the next step on this entrepreneurial journey is to scale. But scaling isn't just about adding more machines or locations; it's about growing intelligently, managing more complexity, and ensuring you don't compromise profitability or quality.

When to Scale

Scaling at the right time is critical. Look for these indicators:

- Consistent Profits: Earning profits consistently, not sporadically.
- Operational Stability: Having streamlined your operational processes effectively.
- Market Demand: Recognizing an apparent and growing demand for your vending products.

Types of Scaling

Scaling can take two primary forms:

- **Vertical Scaling:** Expanding the range of products or services offered through your existing machines. For instance, consider incorporating electronic goods like earphones or phone cables if you're vending snacks.

- **Horizontal Scaling:** Adding more machines, potentially in different locations. This is the traditional notion of "scaling."

Financing the Scale

Scaling your vending business is exciting, but financing this expansion requires strategic decision-making. There are three main avenues, each with its considerations and implications.

- **Bootstrapping:** If your business generates a healthy cash flow, reinvesting that cash back into your business is often the best option. Bootstrapping allows you to scale at your own pace without taking on debt or giving away equity. It's a method where the growth is funded through your existing revenue.
- **Bank Loans:** For those with a solid understanding of their business and at least 12 months of reliable data, securing a bank loan is a viable option. By projecting your business's future performance with accurate financial numbers, you can negotiate a loan that aligns with your growth plans. Ensure the loan terms are favorable, minimizing the risk of excessive debt.
- **Investment from Third Parties:** Choosing outside investment involves bringing in a partner or investor who injects capital into your business. This avenue allows for substantial growth but comes with the trade-off of sharing ownership and decision-making authority. If you choose this

route, think big and be willing to take calculated risks, aligning your visions and expectations with your investor.

13.1: How Many Locations Are Too Many Locations?

Scaling is an integral part of any business strategy, but it's essential to grow smart rather than just fast.

Scaling a vending machine business can be exhilarating. Each new location could add another stream of income. But here's the sobering question: How many locations are too many? Contrary to what you might think, more isn't always better. This will walk you through identifying the optimum scale for your vending machine business.

Understanding Your Limits

Entrepreneurs often fall into the trap of over-expanding, spreading resources thin, and, ultimately, running into operational chaos. Before you plan on adding another pin to your location map, it's vital to understand your current or potential capabilities.

Finding the Breaking Point

Every business has a 'breaking point'—a limit where profits don't just plateau but start to decline. To pinpoint this, track key performance indicators like profit margins, customer satisfaction levels, inventory turnover rates, and employee turnover rates. Negative trends in these metrics may signify you've surpassed your optimal number of locations.

A sweet spot for a small vending operation typically ranges around 25 to 30 machines. If you exceed this, be ready for growing pains. Challenges like operational complexity, increased overhead costs, and quality control issues will arise. It's crucial to confront these challenges head-on, emphasizing efficient processes and unwavering commitment to customer satisfaction.

13.2 Navigating the Challenges

Scaling your vending business is a journey of strategic growth. Here are a few more insights to keep in mind:

Logistical Considerations:

Expanding your vending machine locations means navigating a logistical labyrinth. The distance between locations, reliable transportation availability, and inventory management costs are critical factors. Always keep a watchful eye on these elements as you scale.

The Law of Diminishing Returns:

A fundamental economic principle, the law of diminishing returns, is applicable as you add more locations. Beyond a certain point, each new location contributes less incremental value and can potentially detract value by diverting resources from more profitable locations. Be aware of this principle as you decide on further expansions.

The Cost of Relocation

Prudent business decisions sometimes involve relocating underperforming vending machines. However, it's crucial to recognize the cost implications of downsizing. If a new location isn't yielding the expected results and necessitates a move, prepare for various costs such as contract termination fees, removal and storage expenses for the machines, and new expenses when you relocate.

CHAPTER 14

CASE STUDIES & SUCCESS STORIES

Here is a glimpse of some real-world success stories. Each case is a testament to resilience, adaptability, and the power of innovative thinking, offering a quick peek into the dedication and strategies that have driven these entrepreneurs to overcome challenges and strive in the vending machine business. These examples serve as inspiring blueprints, showcasing how diverse approaches and forward-thinking can carve a path to success in this dynamic industry.

14.1 Wicked Healthy Vending: Healthier Snacking

Idea

Tina Paine, the owner of Wicked Healthy Vending, envisioned a vending machine business that would provide healthy snack options, especially to disadvantaged communities. Her inspiration stemmed from her desire to own a business and her discovery of a company called Naturals2Go, which gave her a jumpstart into the vending industry.

Challenge

Tina had no prior knowledge about the vending industry before starting Wicked Healthy. She had to learn everything from scratch, from stocking to deliveries. Moreover, she faced challenges in the male-dominated vending industry, often perceived as an "old boys' club."

Execution

Starting with just five machines in 2013, Tina expanded her business while working a corporate job until 2018. She then decided to focus on her vending business full-time. She grew her business by about eight machines a year, with about 46 machines across the state by 2021. Tina has two employees and a warehouse to manage the operations, ensuring a smooth workflow and efficient service. She also emphasized professionalism, using her corporate experience to implement contracts and maintain a structured approach to her business.

Success

Wicked Healthy Vending has become one of Massachusetts's fastest-growing healthy vending companies. Tina's unique approach, focusing on providing healthy options and targeting disadvantaged communities, set her apart in the industry. Her commitment to featuring woman-made products and her idea of starting a Women in Vending group further differentiates her business, creating a community and support network for women in the industry.

Key Takeaways

Understanding the Market: It's essential to ask the right questions to ensure a location is profitable. For instance, a location with 100 employees might not guarantee good sales if those employees are not present to buy snacks. Tina's ability to critically assess each potential location has been a key factor in her success.

Professionalism Matters: Tina's background in corporate compliance and her emphasis on contracts and professionalism gave her an edge in the industry.

Continuous Learning: Tina believes in not isolating oneself and stresses the importance of networking, taking classes, and being around other entrepreneurs to share ideas and grow.

Adaptability: Every business has its challenges. For Tina, issues like dollars getting stuck persist even with high-tech machines. However, adapting and addressing these challenges is crucial.

Personal Growth: The entrepreneurship journey has helped Tina grow her business and personally challenged her, making her more confident and resilient.

14.2 FYC Vending: An Answer to a Campus Snack Gap

Idea:

While studying at Georgia State University, Maya Ray observed a lack of quick snack options in her dorm building. After graduating in May 2020 and not securing her desired job in events and marketing, she discovered a course on Twitter about starting a vending machine business, which inspired her to venture into the industry.

Challenge:

Securing profitable locations for the vending machines was a significant challenge. Maya learned the importance of thoroughly vetting placements after opening a location that didn't generate sufficient sales.

Execution:

Maya launched her vending machine business, FYC Vending, in June 2022. Georgia State University, her alma mater, became her first client, and she placed vending machines in the very building she once resided in. To fund her startup costs, Maya used a business credit card. Her initial investment included $6,000 for the first two vending machines and approximately $300 to stock them with snacks and drinks.

Success:

FYC Vending operates five vending machines. By July 2022, Maya had made $32,800 in sales from these machines. Between her launch in June 2022 and July 2022, she achieved $119,200 in sales. Her vending machines at Georgia State University became her most profitable location, requiring restocking three times a week due to high demand.

Key Takeaways:

Research and Planning: Securing a suitable location before purchasing a machine is crucial. Factors like the number of residents, employees, and existing amenities play a role in determining the success of a vending machine in a particular location.

Efficiency: Maya emphasized the importance of efficiency in scaling her business. For instance, she transitioned from weekly shopping at Sam's Club to ordering curbside pickup to save time.

Continuous Learning: Maya plans to launch her course on starting a vending machine business to educate the younger generation about the industry and provide insights for success.

Adaptability: Maya's ability to pivot and adapt, such as selling a location that wasn't profitable and learning from her experiences, played a crucial role in her success.

14.3 Blendid: Tailored Smoothies

Idea:

Blendid's CEO and co-founder, Vipin Jain, was inspired by the replicator machine from the TV franchise "Star Trek," which made food tailored to a person's preferences. He envisioned a similar concept for real-world vending machines.

Challenge:

A significant challenge was creating a vending machine that could produce complex food items, such as smoothies with varying moisture levels from fresh ingredients.

Execution:

Jain launched Blendid, an automated smoothie kiosk. The company now operates 12 units across the U.S., located in places like college campuses and hospitals. They plan to add new units every month throughout the following year. Beyond expanding the concept, Jain's team is developing new offerings.

Success:

Blendid has successfully introduced a modern vending machine concept that offers fresh, customizable smoothies. Jain envisions a future where food service in specific noncommercial venues is fully automated. He imagines a system that can greet guests by name and offer their usual orders tailored to their particular food preferences. Blendid has raised a total of $20 million in investments through a combination of traditional venture capital, strategic investors, and crowdfunding

Key Takeaways:

Innovation: Modern vending machines can offer more than just prepackaged snacks. Companies like Blendid are pushing the boundaries of what automated tech can achieve in the food industry.

Customization: The future of vending might lie in personalization, where machines can recognize individual customers and cater to their specific preferences.

Expansion: Blendid's success showcases the potential for automated food kiosks in various venues, from educational institutions to healthcare facilities.

These stories highlight the adaptability and resilience of entrepreneurs in the vending machine industry. They have found success by understanding their customers' needs and continuously innovating to meet those needs.

CHAPTER 15

FINAL THOUGHTS

As we come to the close of this book, it's important to revisit the essence of what you've learned: vending machines are not a *set-and-forget* business. The notion that you can put a machine out there and start raking in the money is not only unrealistic, but it can set you up for failure. Like any other business, real success in the vending machine business requires strategic planning, dedication, and ongoing management.

Debunking the Myths

Many sell the illusion of vending machines as a form of passive income. But as you've discovered, that's far from the truth. Location selection, machine maintenance, inventory management, and customer service are ongoing tasks that demand time, effort, and investment. This book has aimed to debunk this myth, arming you with the knowledge and tools you need to approach this business realistically.

Putting Knowledge into Action

It's one thing to read a book and quite another to put that knowledge into action. The next step for you is to draft a comprehensive business plan. Consider all the factors we've discussed: cost analysis, location scouting, product selection, maintenance plans, and even an exit strategy should things not go as planned. Having a clear roadmap will help you navigate the challenges that inevitably come up.

Continuous Learning

Research is your ally. Without proper research, navigating the business world is like being blindfolded. Location scouting, market analysis, and understanding customer needs are elements that require thorough research. Constant learning is vital as the vending industry, like any other, is subject to change. Stay ahead by investing in education, attending industry events, networking, and joining vending associations. Get out of the building and never stop learning.

Real Profit Is Achievable

Yes, real profit is achievable, but it won't come without effort. The more strategic and thoughtful you are in your approach, the better your chances of building a vending machine business that not only survives but thrives. Use data to make informed decisions—whether it's sales data from your machines or broader consumer trends.

Your Checklist for Success

- **Business Plan:** Document your goals, estimated costs, revenue models, and operational plan.
- **Research:** Know your market, your competition, and your customers.
- **Legal Compliance:** Ensure you have all the necessary permits and adhere to local regulations.

- **Quality Machines:** Invest in reliable, functional, and visually appealing machines.
- **Sourcing products:** Thoughtfully choose and maintain a diverse product selection from reliable suppliers.
- **Inventory Management:** Keep track of what sells and what doesn't. Be ready to adapt your product offerings.
- **Marketing:** Use data to drive decisions. Attract customers with discounts and branding.
- **Customer Service:** Promptly attend to machine breakdowns, complaints, or refunds.

Final Thoughts

It's time to plan your next steps; remember that while this guide is a roadmap, the journey itself will be uniquely yours. Will there be roadblocks? Absolutely. Could there be detours? Most certainly. But every challenge is an opportunity to learn, adapt, and grow.

Like any other venture, success in the vending machine business is a marathon, not a sprint. Short-term setbacks will happen and shouldn't discourage you. Learn from your mistakes, adjust your strategies, and keep moving forward. Resilience and adaptability are your most valuable assets.

Above all, never stop learning. The business landscape constantly evolves, and staying informed about industry trends will give you a competitive edge. Whether it's a new vending machine type, a shift in consumer preferences, or changing regulations, knowledge equips you for success. Engage with industry reports, attend webinars, or enroll in courses to expand your skill set.

If you're willing to roll up your sleeves and get down to the nitty-gritty aspects of running a business, the vending machine industry is waiting for someone just like you.

Best of luck on your journey!

ABOUT THE AUTHOR

MATT WOODHAMS

Matt Woodhams is the mind behind Vending Bible. His journey with vending started more than 15 years ago. Before that, he worked in technology and retail. Overwhelmed by overhead costs and location fees, he decided to seek a way to sell non-traditional products through vending machines. Little did he know this was a massive challenge that allowed him to learn the secrets of the industry from the best in the business and, in the process, changed his career path and his view on how to sell and why people buy.

Matt's expertise in vending spans a wide array of industries, from traditional snack and beverage machines to cutting-edge technological solutions. He has introduced vending services in various sectors, ranging from dispensing affordable one-dollar snacks to high-end three-hundred-dollar iPads. His journey has led him to secure locations in shopping malls, subways, bus stations, and even in specialized areas requiring a unique vending approach, such as the mining sector and correctional facilities.

Whether navigating the complexities of conventional vending setups or pioneering innovative tech-driven solutions, Matt has experienced the full spectrum of what the vending world has to offer. All of this accumulated knowledge and experience is now channeled into VendingBible.com, an online community he founded to share insights, connect with fellow vending enthusiasts, and help newcomers navigate the often complex world of vending. It's a space for learning, sharing, and growing together, fueled by Matt's passion for vending and his desire to see others succeed in the industry.